My Picture
Goes Here!

What Baptism Means to Me

by Lindsey Shumway

Presented to:

For those times when you want to remember
what baptism means to you.

Presented by:

ISBN 13: 978-1-55517-939-8
ISBN 10: 1-55517-939-8

Published by CFI, an imprint of Cedar Fort, Inc., 925 N. Main, Springville, UT, 84663
Distributed by Cedar Fort, Inc. www.cedarfort.com

Book and Cover design by Nicole Williams

Printed in China

10 9 8 7 6 5 4 3 2 1

Printed on acid-free paper

Congratulations!

Congratulations! You are now a member of The Church of Jesus Christ of Later-day Saints. This has been a very important step in your life, and your baptism day will be a cherished memory for the rest of your life. This book will provide you with a way to record the special feelings you and those you love had on this day. As you travel along the road of life, refer to this book as a reminder of the covenants you have entered into and the blessings you have received.

My Baptism Day

My name is ______________________________

Today is ______________________________

My eighth birthday was on ____________________

I was baptized by ____________________________

At my baptism, these songs were sung ____________

____

These special people spoke ____________________

____

My favorite part of my baptism day was __________

____

____

____

I am thankful to be a member of The Church of Jesus Christ of Latter-day Saints!

my picture goes here

Me on My Baptism Day

Life in My Family

I am a member of the ______________________ family

My mom's name is ______________________________

My dad's name is ______________________________

My siblings' names are ___________________________

____

____

____

We live in ____________________________________

The best thing about my mom is ___________________

____

____

____

The best thing about my dad is ____________________

____

____

____

The best thing about our family is _________________

____

____

____

I am thankful to be part of my family!

I Live Here

my house

me and my family

I ♥ My Family

me and my family

My Family Tree

Me

Dad

Mom

Grandpa

Grandma

Grandpa

Grandma

Great-Grandparents

Great-Grandparents

Life in My Ward

I am a member of the ______________________ Ward

My bishop's name is ____________________________

I am in the __________________________ Primary class

My teacher's name is ____________________________

I have lots of friends at church; their names are ______

____

____

My favorite part of Primary is ___________________

____

____

____

I am thankful to be part of my ward!

me and my friends

laugh
play
love
friends

me and my best friend

What I Learned about Baptism

What the Savior means to me

What the Holy Ghost means to me

What the Book of Mormon means to me

What the First Vision is ______________________

____

____

What the sacrament means to me ______________

____

____

What "accountability" means __________________

____

What "repentance" means ____________________

____

What "remission of sins" means ______________

____

What "covenants" are _______________________

____

What Baptism Means to Joseph Smith

"Baptism is a holy ordinance preparatory to the reception of the Holy Ghost; it is the channel and key by which the Holy Ghost will be administered."

—*Teachings of the Prophet Joseph Smith*, comp. Joseph Fielding Smith (Salt Lake City: Deseret Book, 1976), 148

What Baptism Means to Me

What Baptism Means to President Gordon B. Hinckley

"What a wonderful thing that is, to know that in similitude of death and burial and resurrection of the Son of God we have gone down into the water and been immersed in the water and brought forth out of the water. Baptism is a great and sacred and marvelous ordinance that brings with it the remission of sins, but in larger measure, it is symbolic of the death, burial, and resurrection of our Divine Redeemer."

—*The Teachings of Gordon B. Hinckley,* 2d ed. (Salt Lake City: Deseret Book, 1997), 35

What Baptism Means to My Mom

me and mom

What Baptism Means to President Brigham Young

"All Latter-day Saints enter the new and everlasting covenant when they enter this church. They covenant to cease sustaining, upholding and cherishing the Devil and the Kingdoms of this world. They enter the new and everlasting covenant to sustain the Kingdom of God and no other kingdom. They take a vow of the most solemn kind, before the heavens and the earth, and that, too, upon the validity of their own salvation, that they will sustain truth and righteousness instead of wickedness and falsehood, and build up the Kingdom of God."

—*Discourses of Brigham Young,* comp. John A. Widtsoe (Salt Lake City: Deseret Book, 1954), 160

What Baptism Means to My Dad

me and dad

What Baptism Means to President John Taylor

"When you yielded obedience to the laws of God, obeyed his commandments, and were baptized for the remission of your sins and had hands laid upon you for the reception of the Holy Ghost, you did receive it; and you are living witnesses before God. This is a secret that the world does not comprehend. . . . We are in possession of the principles of eternal life, and are operating for eternity; and then we are operating to build up the Zion of God, where righteousness can be taught, and where men can be protected, and where liberty can be proclaimed to all men of every color, of every creed and of every nation."

—*Teachings of Presidents of the Church: John Taylor* (Salt Lake City: The Church of Jesus Christ of Latter-day Saints, 2002), 70

What Baptism Means to My Siblings

What Baptism Means to President Joseph F. Smith

"I felt in my soul that if I had sinned—and surely I was not without sin—that it had been forgiven me; that I was indeed cleansed from sin; my heart was touched; and I felt that I would not injure the smallest insect beneath my feet. I felt as if I wanted to do good everywhere to everybody and to everything. I felt a newness of life, a newness of desire to do that which was right. There was not one particle of evil left in my soul. I was but a little boy, it is true, when I was baptized; but this is the influence which came upon me, and I know that it was from God."

—*Gospel Doctrine,* 5 ed. (Salt Lake City: Deseret Book, 1971), 96

What Baptism Means to My Grandmother

What Baptism Means to President Harold B. Lee

"Only those who repent and are baptized for the remission of their sins will lay full claim to the redeeming blood of the Atonement."

—*Teachings of Presidents of the Church: Harold B. Lee* (Salt Lake City: The Church of Jesus Christ of Latter-day Saints, 2000), 31

What Baptism Means to My Grandfather

What Baptism Means to President David O. McKay

"In these three instances we have set forth clearly the threefold purpose of the ordinance of baptism:

1. *A rite established by God himself and associated with the eternal principle of righteousness, compliance with the law, therefore, being established to man's salvation.*

2. *An initiatory ordinance—the gateway leading to membership in the fold of Christ.*

3. *A beautiful and sublime symbol typifying the burial of the 'former' man with all his weaknesses and impurities, and the coming forth into a newness of life."*

—*Teachings of Presidents of the Church: David O. McKay* (Salt Lake City: The Church of Jesus Christ of Latter-day Saints, 2003), 201

What Baptism Means to My Aunts

What Baptism Means to Nephi

"I know that if ye shall follow the Son, with full purpose of heart, acting no hypocrisy and no deception before God, but with real intent, repenting of your sins, witnessing unto the Father that ye are willing to take upon you the name of Christ, by baptism—yea, by following your Lord and your savior down into the water, according to his word, behold, then shall ye receive the Holy Ghost; yea, then cometh the baptism of fire and of the Holy Ghost; and then can ye speak with the tongue of angels, and shout praises unto the Holy One of Israel."

—2 Nephi 31:13

What Baptism Means to My Uncles

What Baptism Means to Alma the Elder

"Behold here are the waters of Mormon . . . and now, as ye are desirous to come into the fold of God, and to be called his people, and are willing to bear one another's burdens, that they may be light; yea, and are willing to mourn with those that mourn; yea, and comfort those that stand in need of comfort, and to stand as witnesses of God at all times and in all things, and in all places that ye may be in, even until death, that ye may be redeemed of God, and be numbered with those of the first resurrection, that ye may have eternal life, . . . what have you against being baptized in the name of the Lord?"

—Mosiah 18:8–9

What Baptism Means to My Bishop

What Baptism Means to Moroni

"And now I speak concerning baptism. Behold, elders, priests, and teachers were baptized; and they were not baptized save they brought forth fruit meet that they were worthy of it. Neither did they receive any unto baptism save they came forth with a broken heart and a contrite spirit, and witnessed unto the church that they truly repented of all their sins. And none were received unto baptism save they took upon them the name of Christ, having determination to serve him to the end."

—Moroni 6:1–3

What Baptism Means to My Friends

What Baptism Means to the Apostle Peter

"Repent, and be baptized every one of you in the name of Jesus Christ for the remission of sins, and ye shall receive the gift of the Holy Ghost. For the promise is unto you, and to your children, and to all that are afar off, even as many as the Lord our God shall call."

—Acts 2:38–39

What Baptism Means to My Primary Teacher

I Am Thankful for...

my family

my family

My First Journal